T0368437

FROM THE CITY TO THE WOODS

AN AFRICAN AMERICAN FAMILY'S HUNTING EXPERIENCE

Donny R. Adair

AuthorHouse™
1663 Liberty Drive
Bloomington, IN 47403
www.authorhouse.com
Phone: 1 (800) 839-8640

Published by AuthorHouse 04/28/2015

ISBN: 978-1-5049-0340-0 (sc)
ISBN: 978-1-5049-0341-7 (e)

Library of Congress Control Number: 2015905146

Print information available on the last page.

Table of Contents

Preface

This book is written to encourage African Americans (Black Folks), other people of color (Latinos, Asians, etc.), urban residents or anyone who has not tried them, to experience hunting and target shooting. Many people who would describe themselves by such ethnic and cultural designations have had negative experiences with firearms, have never tried archery, and are afraid to go to the woods or have no desire to kill animals. However, many of you have responded on my website africanamericanhuntingassociation.com and the African American Hunting Association page on Facebook, that you are interested in learning to hunt or shoot, but never had the opportunity. These are the people that I am most interested in helping.

This book is also a wake up call to people who have not thought about hunting or are against it. It shares some positive reasons we hunt which you may not have heard. Maybe I will say something in this book that will help you better understand the mind of a hunter.

Thanks go out to my loving wife who comes from a hunting family and understands the passion I have for it. Love also to my sons who have joined me on hunts and fishing trips. They carried this old mans bags, took pictures and videos which will capture our adventures for all time.

Donny Adair, President
African American Hunting Association, LLC

Kenneth Adair, the author's youngest of 2 sons likes fishing more than hunting, but is a skilled videographer… and he's so cool too!

Why Do People Hunt

There are many reasons why people hunt animals. For some, it's about the preparation and the chase to outsmart an animal in the wild. Others hunt to kill and eat meat and poultry that is organic, leaner than farm-raised and has no man-made additives. Many hunters enjoy developing skills with firearms, archery equipment and traps. You should give some serious thought as to why you are interested in hunting. Does killing bother you? Will you have guilt or regrets if you kill an animal, whether large or small game? Will you consume the meat? How do you feel about hunting for sport or trophies? Will you hunt predators or dangerous game?

Many hunters believe that they are helping to keep nature in balance by making sure that wild animals do not exceed the carrying capacity of the land. In places where we hunt like the state of Mississippi, traffic accidents between vehicles and deer are the number one cause of injuries and deaths. It is an agricultural environment where deer thrive. In southern states like Texas, Florida and out west in California, hogs are overrunning the land and causing havoc on farms, ranches and other rural properties. In those states, and states like Oregon, there is no license required to kill hogs and they can be hunted with any firearm or bow.

A successful hunt is the culmination of applying many outdoor skills. People find hunting interesting because you have to learn about the query you are hunting. The history of the species, the environment, folklore, weather, appropriate hunting methods, game laws, camping, survival skills, first aid, and preservation of harvested game are just some of the topics, which must be addressed. This is what intrigues me the most. I have spent the last 40 years developing a body of hunting knowledge and I have just scratched the surface. It's an on-going challenge. That's why I hunt.

Many hunters got their start by hunting grandpa's or uncle Joe's farm. I, like many African Americans, grew up in an urban environment. I grew up in Portland, Oregon. However, my grandfather, Appleton Charles (A.C.) Adair, who raised me, and my uncle, Bill Anfield, exposed me to the outdoors. I mention him by name because Uncle Bill and Charles Kelly, one of the famous fishing Kelly brothers, were known far and wide as the best Crappie fishermen in the northwest. They were expert fishermen. They focused their efforts on warm water species such as bass, catfish, crappies and blue gills. Of these, the crappie was the most coveted because it is the tastiest fish to many; and, they could be caught by the hundreds when you can locate a feeding school. My uncle always had a firearm, a pistol, but he did not hunt. My grandfather did not hunt either. This is a typical experience of many African Americans growing up in an urban setting.

Uncle Bill Anfield, his 3 sons Billy, James and Carl, Charles Kelly and the day's catch.

The author and cousin Billy Charles Anfield have continued the family fishing tradition for over 50 years. These catfish are from the Snake River on the Oregon-Idaho border.

My introduction to firearms really came from my mother. She worked in clubs at night and carried a .25 caliber semi-automatic pistol in her purse all the time. We were told not to touch it without permission. By the time I was a teenager she had taught me how to safely load and unload the gun and how to fire it. When I got in to college and began purchasing my own guns, "Moms" (family nickname) would ask me to clean her gun and fire it, since she did not get to the country very much. When she passed away in 2008 we discovered a .22 caliber 8-shot revolver on the floor near the head of her bed. There was also a wooden mallet I made in the 8th grade (1964). I guess if the 8 rounds were not enough, she would have beaten an intruder over the head with the mallet. The last of "Moms" gun legacy was the final day we were cleaning her house to sell it. The kids and other family members cleaning the attic discovered a Winchester 94 Lever Action Rifle brand new in the box! Yes, a 30-30 caliber 1968 Buffalo Bill Cody Replica, which had never been fired. Perfect for our hunts in the dense forest of western Oregon for blacktailed deer.

Author Donny Adair with the Winchester left to him by "Moms".

I got my start hunting oddly enough when I was attending college at the University of Oregon in Eugene in 1968. I befriended some brothers (a term of endearment for African American men, who are not necessarily related by blood), who were the Eugene Chapter of the Black Panther Party. They invited me to go hunting with them for deer in the Coast Range Mountains between Eugene, Oregon and the Pacific Ocean. We harvested deer, processed the animals and gave most of the meat to local low income residents, particularly single mothers and elderly.

After college I returned to live in Portland. I could not find any Black hunting partners. So I hunted alone for a few years then quit hunting altogether. I started hunting again when my sons became ages 11 and 12, to expose them to the sport. They had fished with me for years and been exposed to firearms as early as age 6 by their grandfather in Mississippi during their long summer visits.

Donnell, the author's oldest son, followed in his footsteps by harvesting his first Blacktailed buck while attending the University of Oregon in

Why Don't Black People and Others Hunt?

The numbers of all hunters and shooters in the U.S. was shrinking for years. The number of gun owners recently began to increase, even in the face of some terrible tragedies involving deranged gunmen. The reason for this was the political scare and fear campaign, which alleged that President Barrack Obama was going to implement legislation that would decrease access by private citizens to guns and/ or ammunition.

2010 US Census Statistics – Overall Population

- 308 million total population of the U.S.
- 231 million white   74%
- 50.5 million Latino   16%
- 42 million African American   12%
- 17.1 million Asian   5.6%
- 4.2 million Two or more   1%
- 5.2 million Nat. Am/Alaskan   1.7%
- 1.2 million Hawaiian/Pacific Islander 1%

The first question in my mind was what does the demographic data show about the ethnicity of hunters in the United States? According to the most recent data provided by the U.S. Department of Fish and Wildlife here is the breakdown.

Hunters by Race and Ethnicity

- 13.7 million total hunters

- 12.9 million white   94%

- 0.3 million Latino   2.1%

- 0.4 million African American   2.9%

- 0.3 million other   2.1%

- 0.1 million Asian   0.7%

(Source: U.S. Fish and Wildlife Service)

Based on demographic data and trends some of the shooting and hunting industry leaders, such as the National Shooting Sports Foundation (NSSF), have adopted objectives to increase the number of African American and Latino hunters and shooters. I participated in workshops at their Annual Shot Show, which is the largest firearms industry trade show in the world.

Now personally, I think that we (African Americans) may be under counted. Black people are often suspicious of survey questionnaires and don't respond, especially if they would have to divulge things like gun ownership.

Linda Chocolate Adair accompanied the author to the 2015 NSSF Shot Show. Her cosmopolitan looks do not show her upbringing as a country girl in rural Mississippi. She hunted and fished with her father and knows how to process and prepare any kind of wild game.

Reasons African Americans Don't Hunt

The reaction to our website and Facebook page for African American Hunting Association is interesting. While most who blog or post on our sites are experienced hunters, it is obvious that many African Americans have not been exposed to hunting. They want to find hunting partners or clubs in their area. In some cases they have been hunting alone, or with a small group of friends who may be of other ethnic groups. Here is a recent email that is typical:

Howdy Mr. Adair,

As you can see below, my name is Charles Simien; I live in El Paso, TX and hunt Texas, New Mexico and the state of Chihuahua, MX. I usually hunt with Hispanics out here, even though I have one Black hunting buddy, who no longer hunts. Of course on the other side of Texas, I hunt with my family. There are several gun shows in the area where I see a smattering of other Black folk; many do not talk with me, like they would get smeared with blackness. Most Black folk are very urban oriented, don't believe in owning guns, think that eating game is icky and I must be crazy for hunting.

That said, I love hunting and would like to pass the tradition on to other Black youth. Give me a shout out if you would.

Charles L. Simien

Summary of Reasons Why I Think Black people don't hunt.

- We live mostly in urban settings
- Less land ownership
- Media connections with firearms and crime
- Our parents did not introduce kids to the sport
- Economic issues
- Criminal record – cannot own firearms

An obvious reason many Blacks don't hunt is that we live predominantly in cities. During the 20th century we migrated from the plantations and farms of the south to the industrial complex of the northeast, mid-west and western United States. As part of the migration and aging of those who stayed in the rural environment, rural land ownership by Blacks decreased. The access to land by Blacks for hunting is also made more difficult by the national trend in the general population of private landowner restrictions. Many hunters are now leasing hunting rights on private property.

Throughout the United States there are public land hunting opportunities. National Forests, federal wildlife refuges and wilderness areas are open to hunters. Many of the states also have publicly managed wildlife refuges as well. Here in the west many of the timber companies that freely gave access to their forests are now requiring a fee. States like Oregon still have cooperative travel access on hundreds of thousands of acres on private lands.

Many African Americans have had either no experiences with firearms or negative experiences. There is a history of violence that is hard to ignore from Jim Crow lynchings and inner–city drive bye shootings. Recent shooting incidences involving white citizens and police officers shooting and killing Black citizens have been well publicized and are being protested throughout the country. The most asked question I get on my website and blog is "Is it safe to go out in the woods?" Many people say they are scared of "White Folks".

The media's treatment of gun ownership and hunting gives a negative image of African Americans. Most programs on television only depict Blacks with guns involved in criminal activity. The absence of African Americans in positive settings with firearms, such as target shooting or hunting, is noted. In fact, some say the TV channels portray hunting as a "red neck sport". Rarely is there an article or even a picture of an African American hunting in regional or national magazines. In the November 2010 issue of Outside Magazine there was a 4-page article on the African American Hunting Association I founded. It had a picture of my son Donnell Chocolate Adair in a Mississippi Swamp that we were hunting near the home of my in-laws in the Delta. We believe that was the first national article ever on Black hunters.

Recently in the 2014 November/December issue of Bear Hunting Magazine, my friend Dante Zuniga-West, a young up and coming outdoor writer, was published. He and a friend harvested a monster-sized Black Bear in Oregon's Coast Range of Mountains in April of 2014. His blog, The Backwoods Blaxican, profiles his outdoors experiences and contains some outstanding outdoor photography as well.

Many African Americans, being raised in the urban environment, do not get introduced to hunting by their parents. Many states, like my home state of Oregon, do not hold hunter education classes in the inner city. However, hunting clubs are increasing the opportunity for inner-city kids to get exposed to all manner of outdoor experience. You will have to investigate your local area to see what gun clubs, archery clubs and youth clubs are doing to provide hunter education and orientation.

Some Black gun hunters and non-hunters have declined to take up archery in states, which do not allow you to carry a pistol as a back up for safety. Some say the reason is not that they think a bear might get them; but they fear people. I have to confess that I have hunted in rural areas in the west close to where white supremacists live. My sons and I are heavily armed when we do. I have said to them when we split up sometimes, "If you come upon a group of guys at a camp fire and it is in the shape of a cross; don't stop and ask to warm up your hands at their fire".

Another major reason that African Americans don't hunt is the cost, especially if you are doing it as a hobby or sport. My wife grew up in rural Mississippi. Her father brought home wild game, including small game like squirrels and raccoons (coons is really the correct pronunciation) and large game like deer and wild hogs. It only cost him the price of a used gun and some .22 caliber bullets, which were used by this expert marksman. An old pickup or car was the only vehicle needed, if any.

This is the typical experience of people who were raised or live in the country, regardless of race or ethnicity. Even if you didn't live there you may have gotten your first hunts on your grandpa's, uncles/aunt's or other relative's farm or property. Often the fish and wildlife rules may have been stretched to feed the family. My wife grew up thinking that you only hunted at night. I found out why when we visited my in-laws in the fall years ago. Each night my father-in-law would disappear in to the woods just before dark and return well after dark with some kind of game to be skinned.

Percy Chocolate of Fitler, Ms, and author (son-in-law) Donny Adair

Percy Chocolate with a "Coon" he harvested on a cool November night.

The costs associated with hunting may vary, but you can bet you are going to have to invest some bucks if you want to do it legally, safely and effectively. You will have to obtain at least one firearm (probably a rifle) or bow, ammunition and proper clothing for the weather and game you will be hunting. If you select archery as your method of hunting, you will need to purchase a bow, arrows, a range finder and a good case. I prefer a hard case, for protecting my bow. You will need a vehicle or you will have to contribute to transportation if you travel with a buddy. Most importantly, you must purchase the required license and tags from the state or country that you will hunt. In the year that I hunted Oregon, Alaska and Mississippi I spent several hundred dollars just on the papers in my back pocket. I will discuss the costs of hunting more in some of the following chapters on how to jumpstart your hunting hobby.

Last but not least, one of the reasons that African Americans don't hunt is because they have a criminal record, are on parole or probation, and may be prohibited from possessing a firearm. A disproportionate number of African Americans have had some involvement with the criminal justice system as a juvenile or an adult. However, in many states, like my home state of Oregon, there is a statute that allows you to petition the court to be allowed to possess a firearm for hunting. This will cost you a filing fee, which is currently about $275.00.

Those are some of the reasons that Black people have shared with me and that I have discovered why they haven't considered or tried the hunting and shooting sports that I, and many people, enjoy so much. I'm sure you have heard many others.

Is hunting for you? Make up your mind.

This will be a short chapter, the reason being is that this may be a point at which you $%@# or get off the proverbial pot. Hunting is not for everyone. Although my family and I believe you should eat what you kill; I understand and accept hunting for sport and trophies. As long as the game meat is not wasted (which is required by law) and given to someone who can use it, I'm cool with people hunting for sport or trophies. Also, I encourage people to try target shooting with gun or bow. It can be fun and offers competitive challenges. I shoot trap with my 12-gauge shotgun at least 2 or 3 times a month. I don't advocate to anyone that they should hunt. However, I do share my love for guns, bows, shooting and the challenge of harvesting something good for the table.

Hunter education is the first thing you need to do!

It is imperative that anyone who wants to learn how to hunt or to shoot to get some instruction from a competent instructor. All youth under the age of 18 must take a hunter education course, pass a test and be certified by a state wildlife agency to legally hunt big game. It is a good idea, even if the youth is only going to hunt small game. Also hunter education may be required of young adults over 18 born after a certain date. Check your state regulations. In addition hunters of any age are required to have hunter-ed certification to purchase out of state licenses in some states. If you are traveling out of state to hunt, check before you leave. Most states, like our home state of Oregon, list the hunter-ed certification right on your hunting license. So if you travel, take your home state license with you as proof.

I took and passed the highest level of courses to obtain a certification of Master Hunter. That allows me access to some exclusive draws hunts. For example, I drew a late season hunt for a cow elk in northwestern Oregon, which allows me to hunt until mid-March. There are only 10 or 11 of these tags available to Master Hunters only. Oregon has an emergency hunt program. When you sign up by county to help control animals, which are damaging property or livestock, Master Hunters' names are listed at the top of the list. They receive opportunities to conduct emergency hunts first.

My final and most important reasons why hunter education is such an important issue are safety, safety and safety. Oh did I say safety? Don't put a firearm in your hand if you don't know how to safely use it. Also, you need to understand the responsibility that goes with firearm safety, including keeping others from accessing and using your firearm(s) without your consent. Bows are just as deadly and should be regarded as a weapon just as you would a gun. All weapons should be lock and stored properly in a safe or at least use trigger locking devices so they cannot be fired by anyone without your consent.

To access hunter education courses you should contact the state fish and wildlife agency in your state. All of them have websites with complete information. Also many of the state agencies allow you to take the hunter education course and test on line. There are private groups that promote hunter education throughout the country. One such organization is the International Hunter Education Association (IHEA). Contact them at ihea.com.

Also, consider in this modern era of the Internet and social media, conducting a comprehensive Internet search. Just type in the hunting subject and many choices will pop up. Social media is just full of sites for hunters. They include manufacturers, retailers, outfitters, clubs, etc. Youtube and other video sources offer some of the most in-depth short programs, which demonstrate how to hunt. My disclaimer here is that some of it is very good and some of it is bad, or at least inaccurate. My Youtube video channel is AAHUNT.TV. My most watched video is How to Use a Climbing Treestand. It has about 20,000 views so far. There are also some videos posted on the African American Hunting Association page on Facebook.

Make it a family affair

Like a lot of people who have contacted me through my website (aahunt.com), and my Facebook Page African American Hunting Association, I had difficulty finding hunting partners upon my return home to Portland, Oregon after attending college. I did hunt alone for a while and occasionally hunted deer in western Oregon with a friend from Salem. He was a state police officer and a skilled marksman and hunter. Because we lived in 2 different cities, it was hard to get together for a hunt very often. At the time I commuted to my job working in executive service in state government from Portland to Salem (47 miles) 5 days a week. Hooking up with my hunting partner in Salem on weekends and traveling to hunt the coast mountain range was just too much. Then I quit hunting altogether.

My sons were born when I was in my mid-thirties. When they became 11 and 12 years old I decided to expose them to hunting. I enrolled us all in hunter education and we took classes at the Tri-County Gun Club in the suburb of Sheraton, Oregon in the spring of 1998. This was no small task and illustrates the difficulties inner city residence still face when trying to find a hunter-ed class near them. This shooting facility is located about 35 miles southwest of North Portland where we live. In addition, my oldest son was in Outdoor School at a camp about 15 miles east of Portland. These were late afternoon/evening sessions (2) during the week for classroom. The shooting part of the class was on a Saturday and my sons Outdoor School had concluded. So I had to drive to camp East of Portland near Sandy, Oregon, then to the gun club, back to camp and finally home for 2 nights. Finally the last trip was just from Portland to Sherwood and return. I probably drove 200 plus miles. Thank God they passed the test, especially Kenny, who was only eleven! Thank goodness you can take the class and test online, but you still have to find a club to take the hands on shooting portion of the class.

The first hunts with my sons, Kenny (age 11), and Donnell (age 12) on Sauvie Island, Oregon.

Equipment…what should you buy?

When it comes to buying equipment go slow and be frugal, even if you have a lot of money. I am going to talk about everything but weapons in this section.

In general the clothing you will need to hunt should be dictated by the weather you expect to experience. You will want to stay cool in warm weather and warm in cold weather. You will definitely need to stay dry in wet weather. Manufacturers and retailers of hunting apparel insist that you need the latest camouflaged, scientifically developed, breathable, waterproof outfit. Truth be told, that old jacket and pants you been wearing might just do fine. My father-in-law has killed more deer than anyone I have ever met. He just wore the clothes he worked the farm in. He never used a cover scent of any kind. He just played the wind.

If you want to look good, stay concealed and reduce your scent, then go ahead and get the best hunting clothing you can afford. You will find that every store has clearance racks or a room. Usually the bargains can be had at the end of the season. For, example the best time to by a turkey vest would be in late May or early June at the conclusion of the spring season.

As far as waterproof clothing; boots should be light as possible with the right tread pattern for the terrain; jackets and pants should be quiet when you walk or rub against the brushes or tree branches.

The two (2) pieces of clothing I recommend that you do wear when hunting big game are a blaze orange hat and vest/jacket. Its not required in every state, so check the regulations. When we hunt in Mississippi or the state of Washington blaze orange is required. In some states it cannot be a black and orange camo pattern. In Oregon the state recently adopted regulations, which require youths under age 18 to wear at least one blaze orange article of clothing, jacket or a hat, which is visible 360 degrees on their person. Turkey hunters are the only hunters who are not required to wear blaze in some states, but again you must check the regulations for the state you will hunt.

I am not going to discuss some of the other costs in this book, which is primarily designed for beginners. However, you should at least be thinking about other costs, because you may have to save for them. Some of those items include four wheel drive vehicles, camping equipment, outfitter and guide fees, air fare, motel, gas, oil, etc.

Expenses, which are mandatory, include license fees and tags required by state fish and wild life agencies and the federal government. Here is an example of what you would have to pay in 2015 in my home state of Oregon.

Juvenile Licenses	Resident	Nonresident
Juvenile Sports Pac (Combination Angling/Hunting/Shellfish License, Combined Angling Harvest Tag, Validation for Upland Bird and Waterfowl hunting, General or Controlled Buck Deer or Controlled Antlerless Deer, General or Controlled Elk, General Cougar, General or Controlled Bear and Spring Turkey Tag)	$55	---
Annual Juvenile Hunter	$14.50	$27.50
Juvenile Turkey Tag	$10.50	$10.50

Hunting Licenses	Resident	Nonresident
Sport Pac (Combination Angling/ Hunting/Shellfish License, a Combined Angling Harvest Tag, a Validation for Upland Bird and Waterfowl hunting, plus a General or Controlled Buck Deer, General or Controlled Elk, General Cougar, General or Controlled Bear and Spring Turkey Tag)	$164.75	---
Combination – hunting and fishing	$58.00	---
Hunting License	$29.50	$148.50
Senior Citizen Combination License (70 and older, Oregon resident for 5 years)	$21.50	---
Senior Citizen Hunting License (70 and older, Oregon resident for 5 years)	$13.75	---
Three Day Nonresident Bird Hunting	---	$26.50
Permanent Disabled Veteran Combination License	Free	---
Permanent Pioneer Combination License	Free	---

Big Game Tags	Resident	Nonresident
Pronghorn Tag	$44.50	$341.50
Black Bear Tag	$14.50	$190.50
Bighorn Sheep Tag	$122.50	$1,308.50
Cougar Tag	$14.50	$14.50
Deer Tag	$24.50	$383.50

Elk Tag	$42.50	$508.50
Disabled Vet/Pioneer – Elk Tag	$22.25	N/A
Rocky Mountain Goat Tag	$122.50	$1,308.50
Controlled Hunt Applications		
Big Game Controlled Hunt Application	$8.00	$8.00
Game Bird Controlled Hunt Application	$2.00	$2.00

Upland Game Bird and Waterfowl
Upland Game Bird License Requirements
Upland Game Bird Resources
Waterfowl Resources
Hunting Tags Permits and Validations

Pheasant Tag (Denman, E.E. Wilson, Fern Ridge, Sauvie Island)	$17.00	$17.00
Turkey Tag	$22.50	$77.50
Game Bird Permit/Reservation (Fern Ridge, Klamath Falls, Sage Grouse, Sauvie Island)	$4.00	$4.00
Upland Game Bird Stamp (Validation*)	$8.50	---
Waterfowl Bird Stamp (Validation*)	$11.50	---
Nonresident Bird Stamp (Validation*)	---	$38.50
Wildlife Area Bird Hunt Reservation/Permit	$4.00	$4.00

ODFW Wildlife Area Parking Permits

Fifteen ODFW Wildlife Areas require a parking permit: Coyote Springs, Denman, E.E. Wilson, Elkhorn, Fern Ridge, Irrigon, Jewell Meadows, Klamath, Ladd Marsh, Phillip W. Schneider, Power City, Sauvie Island, Summer Lake, White River, and Willow Creek Wildlife Areas. $7.00 (One Day Pass) $22.00 (Annual Pass)

Small Game Hunting and Trapping

Small Game Resources

Furbearer License	FEE
Resident Furtaker's License	$47.00
Nonresident Furtaker's License	$352.00
Resident Hunting License for Furbearers	$22.00
Resident Juvenile Furtakers License (Age 14-17)	$17.00
Juveniles younger than 14	See license requirements above

As you can see hunting costs can be significant depending on the game you select to hunt. I advise beginners to just select 1 to 3 types of game to hunt. An example would be turkey in the spring, deer and waterfowl in the fall. It's your call and your wallet. I have on occasion bought a license or tag and then decided not to hunt. There are no refunds!

Hunting Methods

I learned four (4) different ways to hunt. They are stand hunting, still hunting, spot and stalk and drives. All but drives can be done alone. Drives require 2 or more hunters working together. Let me also say that, while I have hunted alone at times, it is much safer to hunt with at least one other hunting buddy. I urge you "don't hunt alone". Besides being much safer it is a lot of fun to share the challenges and experiences of hunting and the outdoors with someone else.

Stand hunting is simply taking a stationary position and letting the game come to you or cross an area where you can shoot it before it detects you. You can stand or sit anywhere you believe the game will not see you on the ground behind natural cover or a man made ground blind. I have done both successfully. You also may elect to sit in a tree stand above the game. This may help you to get your scent above the animal you are hunting. I have used ladder tree stands and climbing tree stands and find them both effective and safe if you take the proper precautions. This includes using a safety harness system to prevent falling to the ground suffering a serious injury and even death! There are also man-made box blinds, usually constructed next to food plots, which are also popular and safe. The other kind of blinds used include, waterfowl blinds over or near water, dugouts and individual pop-up style blinds you can lay down in. Taking a stand is an excellent way for anyone with limited mobility due to health or age issues to be able to participate in the sport of hunting. There are programs that assist people who have been wounded in the service of our country that often use stand hunting techniques. Also, as I have gotten older (I'm 64 years old now) I have had to recognize that my physical abilities have changed.

Still hunting is a term for walking very, very slowly through the woods in an effort to see the quarry before it sees you. When I say slow walking I mean really so slow that sometimes you may not cover even 100 yards in a half hour. The key is to walk like a game animal looking around in every direction after 1 or 2 steps. Each step you take will give you a new view of the area being hunted. Also game such as deer will sometimes let you get very close to them, then get nervous and bolt in to the open where you can get a shot. You may also get an opportunity to shoot game while it is bedded down. Still hunting may involve following tracks and trails and other sign such as droppings (feces), rubs and scrapes on trees and hair. In addition to your sight you may be able to smell scent left by animals. For example, when you come upon a deer bedding area your nose will definitely let you know if the animals have been there recently. To effectively hunt on the ground, either stand, still hunting or stalking you must control your scent and/or play the wind correctly. You should make sure the wind is blowing in your face or across so that your scent is not blown to the animal you are walking toward. If the wind is at your back, wait until the wind changes or change hunting direction if possible. Most big game animals can smell many times better than a human.

Stalking and spot and stalking methods are for hunters who like to get out there and go after the game. Usually the hunter will cover ground at a steady pace until the game is seen. Then a plan is made to get closer to within shooting range. Use of sight is the key. Often this requires the use of good optics including binoculars and/or a spotting scope. While a riflescope will also allow the hunter to see with much better clarity and greater distance than the naked eye, never use a riflescope to spot game. You could accidently shoot someone. Once the game is spotted with other optics, then, and only then, use your scope to shoot. Hunters should be in good physical condition to stalk game. You may have to walk and climb for miles. Depending on the terrain it can be grueling. You may also be hunting at higher altitudes than you are used to. The thin air could cause you to suffer from altitude sickness. It is wise to work out at least 3 days per week and eat a healthy diet to hunt safely and comfortably. It will be a lot more fun if you are in shape.

Using the technique of driving animals out in to the open, where members of a hunting party can shoot them takes coordination and patience. Two (2) or more hunters can conduct a drive, but usually there are a lot more hunters that participate. Hunters are broken up in to drivers and standers. The drivers walk through the woods and drive the game to standers strategically placed ahead of the drivers. The standers will shoot the game without shooting towards the drivers. My son Donnell and I have not been very successful conducting 2-man drives. However, I have been on 2 drives in the Mississippi Delta, which were both successful. I didn't get a shot, but the animals were driven from a thicket on a farm near Anguila, and a beautiful 8-point buck was harvested on one memorable hunt. I was in awe of the courage of those young men, some of them teenagers, who walked through those snake infested woods to drive the deer in to an open field. Make sure you have a good leader for any drive you attempt. Darnell "Don" Berry, who has taught and mentored many hunters in the Rolling Fork, Mississippi area was our host and coordinated the drives I participated in.

This is Don Berry on his family farm near Anguila, Mississippi.

The Mississippi Boyz – hunters with a beautiful 8-point Whitetail buck after a successful drive/hunt near Anguila in the Mississippi Delta.

Guns and Optics for beginners

Before you buy anything try out as many different firearms as you can. Go to a shooting range or club. Get help from competent trainers, friends and mentors. Shoot different caliber rifles, pistols and shotguns. Start with lighter shooting calibers such as .22 rimfire. Using .22's in the summer to keep up your skills is called plinking. These are easy to shoot and light on the pocketbook. I spend about 5 cents a bullet. This caliber of bullet has been difficult to get over the last 2 or 3 years because of hoarding due to the aforementioned Obama scare. However, .22-caliber ammunition has recently begun to be more available. Some of the larger sporting goods chains recently advertised sales of .22's. Hopefully you can afford to have a .22 for practice and small game, in addition to a big game rifle and/or shotgun. It's a great tool to introduce your kids to target shooting. My sons, daughters and granddaughters all shot my .22 rifle. You may want to purchase a handgun/pistol also.

The author's granddaughter, Tiana Rasin, fires the pump .22 rifle.

First let's discuss rifles. In addition to choosing a caliber you need to select the kind of action you like. The action of the rifle is the mechanism that loads and then ejects the cartridge. By the way there are 3 basic parts to rifle ammunition the case, the powder and the bullet or projectile. Together they are called cartridges. Many people just call them bullets, but just so you know… The most popular rifle actions for hunting are bolt action, semi-automatic, and lever action. There are also rifles that break open like a shotgun and a few pump or slide action models. Many shooters believe that the bolt action is the most accurate. Lever action rifles and semi-automatic rifles provide faster follow-up shots. Most hunters and shooters agree that whatever action you use in the field, try to make the first shot count. You must answer the question "what is the action that I can shoot the best".

In addition to getting a .22 caliber, if you are going to hunt mid-size and large game such as deer, antelope, elk, moose and black bear, you must have a gun that will quickly and humanely dispatch the animal. There are some minimum caliber requirements required by state fish and game agencies. For the requirements in my home state consult the Oregon Department of Fish and Wildlife Big Game Regulations available at any license point of sale agent or go online to http://www.dfw.state.or.us/resources/hunting/big_game/regulations/weapons.asp . There is a comprehensive chart listing the minimum caliber for rifles, handguns, shotguns and muzzleloaders, which can be used to hunt pronghorn antelope, deer, elk, black bear & cougar, big horn sheep & rocky mountain goat and western grey squirrel. Basically what it boils down to, for big game you must shoot at least a .243 Winchester caliber rifle. This would be fine on small deer, such as the Blacktailed Deer of western Oregon or an antelope on the eastern side of the state. However, if you want a multi-purpose rifle you should consider larger calibers such as .270, .280, 7MM-08, 7MM Magnum, .30-.30, .30-.06, 300 Winchester Magnum or 300 Winchester Short Magnum (WSM).

Author on a late season emergency elk hunt in the Southern Willamette Valley authorized by the Oregon Department of Fish and Wildlife.

I am not an expert. I'm more of a hunting enthusiast. I can't recommend an action or caliber of rifle, because I don't know what you are going to hunt and all the other variables that should go in to your decision. I can share with you my experience. My first hunting rifle was a .30-.30 caliber lever action with a 4X scope. It was used and I purchased it from a friend. I won't say what the brand was because they are not paying me to advertise for them. It was ok for hunting the thick brush of western Oregon's Coast Range Mountains. It was accurate and easy to shoot out to about 150 yards. I used it to qualify for the state's Master Hunter Certification shooting test. My current deer rifle is a lever action in 7MM-08, topped with a good 2X-7X-40mm Leupold brand scope. I have cleanly killed deer and 2 cow elk with this rifle. I also have and use a bolt action in 300 (WSM), with a good quality 3X –9X – 40mm scope, which is what I take to Alaska, Montana and any where else there may be dangerous game such as Grizzly or Brown Bears. Also I would use this rifle to hunt bull elk in the future. But there is a video of me shooting a Cow Elk in Idaho with my 7MM-08. One shot through vitals at 182 yards spun the animal around and she died instantly on the spot. The bullet went clean through. Some say this caliber is too light for elk, but I have a rule, which is "Don't fight success!"

Author harvested his 2nd cow elk in Northern Idaho.

When it comes to optics, if you are going to shoot any distance with your hunting rifle beyond 25 or 30 yards, you should consider mounting a scope of some kind. Spend enough money to get a good scope with multi-coated lenses that do not fog up in cold or wet weather.

I am also trying to harvest a deer or cow elk with my .44 magnum revolver handgun. The first couple of years I had it I topped it with a very good 2X -20mm scope. It was very accurate to 100 yards but slow target acquisition on multiple shots. I am demonstrating a new reflex sight this year for a company. It is much less bulky and features much quicker target acquisition. Man that electronic red dot is easy to see, but it's not as accurate as the 2x. In the brush of Western Oregon it is perfect for deer and even elk at 75 yards or less. I have other handguns for self-defense and target shooting. I like to carry a side arm with me at all times when I am in the woods. That's just me.

The last firearm I will discuss is probably the most versatile. It's the shotgun. The shotgun is a smooth bore barreled firearm that uses ammunition (shells) filled with small round pellets called shot. The size of the bore is called the gage. The smaller the number, the bigger the shotguns barrel. Shotguns come in 10, 12, 16, 20, 28 and 410 gage barrels. The most popular are the 12, 20 and 410 gage shotguns. The size of the shot you use would vary depending on the use. Shot sizes range from the smallest #9 to the largest 00. The smaller sizes #7-1/2 to #9 would be used at a gun club to shoot trap, skeet or sporting clay; and also to hunt small birds such as quail or dove. Larger sizes of shot maybe #6 and #5 would be used to hunt larger birds like pheasants and turkeys; and to hunt small game such as squirrels and rabbits. Shot sizes #4, #3, #2, or BB would be used for ducks and geese to get out to further distances. Sizes #1 Buckshot, 00 Buckshot is for large game or self-defense at short ranges. Last but not least is the slug, which is a shell, packed with a lead or other single metal projectile. In some of the mid-western states that have flat terrain have shot gun only rules, which requires firearm hunters to use shotguns with buckshot or slugs. Buckshot and slugs are often used when hunters conduct drives to make the hunt safer.

Author attended an ODFW pheasant clinic at E.E Wilson Wildlife Area in Adair, Oregon (no relation). Below the author took this wild turkey with a 12-gage shotgun.

Archery Equipment

This will also be a short chapter because I just purchased and began using a compound bow just 2 years ago. Like others I want to take the challenge of having to get closer to the game to get a killing shot. That's what bow hunting offers. To be honest I would have tried archery hunting a long time ago, but the fish and wildlife agency in my state would not let us carry a firearm as a back-up weapon. Where we hunt we always see signs of black bear and cougars. Incidents between predators and humans are increasing. Several years ago as result of the work of the statewide hunters organization, a state attorney general's opinion regarding carrying firearms, clarified that the legislature determines what firearms can be carried, and fish and wildlife has authority to determine what weapons can be used to harvest game. So now hunters may legally to carry a sidearm when archery hunting. You should check the regulations in the state that you plan to hunt.

Also, I have discovered in this short time that archery is a lot of fun and after the initial investment for bows arrows and case, its very inexpensive. When I am competing with my son he often reminds me "Its cheaper than a box of bullets". I am a member of a private archery club and a public archery range.

Recurve bows, long bows, compound bows and crossbows are the choices for archers. I have a compound bow. The technology of these modern versions of the traditional bow, drop the pulled weight by about 25% at full draw. This allows the shooter to hold full draw easier and longer. This helps the shooter to be more accurate. My son and I were able to shoot accurately out to 50 yards in just a few short months.

My friend Sharon Ross purchased a bow last year. She took a comprehensive bow hunting course from the National Bowhunter Education Foundation. She practices with me regularly.

Sharon Ross on a public archery range in Fairview, Oregon.

Honestly, I have been so happy with my compound bow that I have not tried shooting Recurve or long bows. I did shoot a crossbow, and I absolutely loved it. However, they are not legal to hunt with in my state. Maybe by the time I write my next book I will have more information to share with you about the sport of archery. As with the other aspects of hunting I encourage you to go to sporting goods stores, archery clubs, and shooting ranges for more information. People at the ranges are very friendly and helpful. You will make new friends, and perhaps even find new hunting partners.

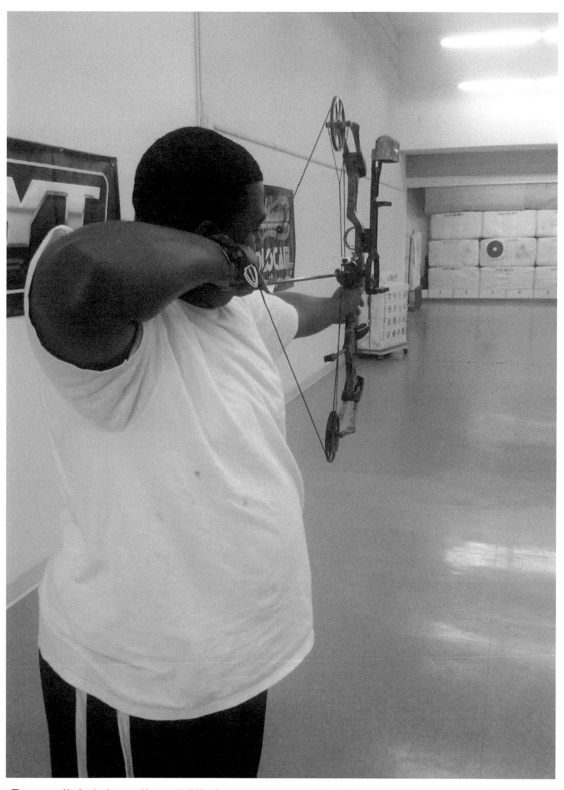

Donnell Adair pulls a 70lb bow very easily. The minimum requirement for deer is 40lbs. The minimum requirement for hunting elk is 50lbs.

Other Essential Gear

The author took a stand on the ground underneath some trees overlooking a clearing in Western Oregon. He was able to comfortably sit from dawn to dusk, occasional leaving the blind to still-hunt the dense forest.

When you take to the forest to hunt you should carry at least a daypack. You must be able to survive if something happens and you have to spend the night. Even if it is just a day hunting trip, you must stay nourished and hydrated. You will need to take some food and water. Other tools to consider include a chair, extra ammunition, a first aide kit, binoculars and/or a spotting scope, camera, tripod, a whistle, game calls, a space blanket, knife, saw and some fire starting tools that will work even in wet conditions. Take your phone, a compass or GPS unit, map and walkie-talkies if you are hunting with a buddy.

Practice makes perfect.

To become good at any sport you must practice. You must learn how to do the things the right way. This means you will need the help of instructors, experienced shooters, mentors and other hunters to help you become competent. If you don't have friends, then pay for instruction or join clubs that mentor shooters. Get to the range as often as you can. Don't go to the range once or twice a year to site in your gun and then go to the field. It's just not safe.

Donny and Donnell Adair on the archery range again!

Finding hunting partners and forming relationships

The task of finding hunting partners is difficult for African Americans, people of color and urban residents. The lack of trust between whites and blacks goes way back in American history. On my blog and Facebook page people around the country still fear that if they go in to the woods with white strangers that some evil tragedy may befall them.

To combat the fear there are several suggestions I have. First seek out Black shooting, hunting and archery clubs. This is a difficult task and I am not sure why. I sent out a call on my Facebook in 2014 asking Black clubs to send me some information to show prospective new members their way. Only 2 clubs responded. Now you have to remember we are talking about hunting. So I believe that there are some reasons why folks don't want to divulge that they hunt. Perhaps they don't want people to know they have weapons. They don't want to share their coveted hunting areas, where they have successfully harvested game. It is true, especially in the southern United States where most of the Black hunters live; white people are buying or restricting hunting rights at a rapid rate. The hunting lease industry is booming. At my in-laws house in rural Mississippi, over time, they have become surrounded by food plots and hunting stands. Almost all the land black people traditionally hunted in the neighborhood is now restricted to those who can pay thousands of dollars to hunt.

There are still ways to connect with other black hunters and I also urge you to make new friends from other cultures. I have developed to some good white hunting buddies. In the 21st century many people are open to interracial friendships.

You definitely can find new hunting partners through the Internet. Randall "Rooster" Wilson of North Carolina contacted the author Donny Adair on the African American

Hunting Association page on Facebook. He invited Donny and son Donnell to join he and friend Sam Frazier, also of North Carolina, on a Black Bear hunt and Halibut fishing trip in Alaska. The four hunters spent five days aboard a boat named the Naughti Lady, owned by Bob's Trophy Charters, Homer Alaska. Three of the four hunters Randall, Donnell, and Sam harvested bears on the Kenai Peninsula, and all four caught their limit of 6 species of fish from the Pacific Ocean.

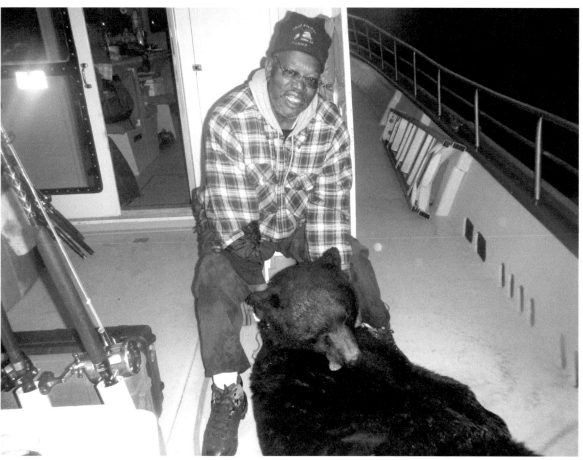

Author Donny Adair caught this unusually large Yellow Eye Rockfish. The Boat Captain estimated the fish to be a hundred years old.

Now this was not a hunt for beginners, but if you went with experienced hunting partners and hunted in pairs as we did, you probably would be safe. It is sometimes called a gentleman's hunt. However, the Captain who transported us from in the Zodiac from the 45-foot vessel named the Naughti-Lady, could not assist us to hunt or retrieve our game in any way. We hunted the Kenai Peninsula switching partners for 3 days. Everyone killed a bear accept for me. I concentrated on taking pictures and video after my son harvested a nice bear. I was paying his way and I did not have the budget for 2 taxidermy bills. No worries. I was happy for him and we share the beautiful bearskin rug. We also took home over a hundred pounds of Halibut from this wonderful visit to the "last frontier".

Sam's bear

One of the most exciting moments of the Alaska adventure for me was Samuel Frazier killing the largest of the 3 bears harvested on this hunting and fishing expedition. It was last of the 3 days we could hunt. When we were fishing that afternoon Sam lamented how he would be satisfied with just taking home some fish. Rooster and Donnell had already taken good bears, but Sam had gotten sick the second night of the hunt. He had an upset stomach and leg cramps that night after a long hunt/walk with me earlier in the day. I told him if he felt better that evening I would go out with him again and together we would get him his bear. That's exactly what we did!

On the final cruise in the Zodiac, at about 10:00 o'clock in the evening, the captain took us into a little creek channel. It was still bright enough to see well in the land of the midnight sun. There on a grassy knoll just out from the rocky shore was a beautiful Black bear feeding. The captain whispered to Sam "You'll have to shoot him from the boat." Sam raised his 270 Weatherby Magnum and fired two shots. As he said later, the second shot was not needed. (It is legal to shoot bear from a boat in Alaska. Be sure to check the regulations for the state you are hunting)

Donnell Adair took a black bear on the Kenai Peninsula in Alaska.

Outfitters and Guides

One of the best ways to learn how to hunt is to purchase the services of hunting guides and outfitters. Experienced outdoorsmen and outdoorswomen are worth their weight in gold, but you won't have to pay that much. I'm not taking about going on an expensive safari to begin with. I'm suggesting that if you want to hunt waterfowl for instance, you could get a good guide to take you out for a day to his blind or property. Services and instruction may include learning how to deploy and shoot over decoys, call in birds and retrieve them. You could often get a limit of ducks or geese (my guide gives me his birds as well), learn how to train your dog to retrieve and the guide may also help you clean the birds for as little as $100 -$150. What a deal!

Big game guides and outfitters cost considerably more, but again it may be worth it to learn how to hunt the right way.

Donnell Adair and Rian Strong owner of North Unit Hunt Club – Sauvie Island, Oregon. Rian is one of the best waterfowl callers in the country. Donnell began hunting with him in 1998 at the age of 12.

Preserving your game in the field

If you want to make great table fare out the animals you shoot, then it starts with what you do in the field. The entrails should be removed as quickly as possible from all animals as soon as you kill them. If you don't, you risk tainting the flavor of your game when cooked. Next you need to get the skin off everything except birds, and get the meat (either boned or not) in to game bags to protect it from parasites, dirt and moisture. There are different preferences on whether to skin the animal first or gut it first and I have done it both ways. The most important thing to know is that you must cool the meat and keep it cool and dry. If you can get it on ice after the meat has some time to age, that's great. When you attend hunter education you will find out more about how to preserve your game.

Hunters Emile and Victor near Rosharon, Texas are experts at processing wild game.

Enjoy the great table fare of the outdoors

I have asked my wife, who has eaten and prepared wild game her entire life to consider writing a cookbook. I am a good cook myself, but I am not going to divulge any specific recipes in this book. However, here are some principals and preferences that I have derived from my experiences. Most wild game is leaner than domestically raised animals. Therefore when frying the game consider cooking in some kind of oil such as olive oil or vegetable oil. Also dredging meat in flour is a good idea. Don't over cook the meat. It will get tough and dry. Consider adding some pork or other fatty meat to your wild game when making sausage, jerky or pepperoni. Use the services of a professional butcher until you obtain the right equipment and knowledge to make wild game products. Then "do it yourself".

Have a great time consuming some of the best tasting organic protein. While you are doing it, relive the story of how you harvested, processed and prepared this wonderful renewable food source.

Venison sausage and Southern fried Potatoes – Yum!

Conservation and Ethics

I don't want to preach to anyone about morals or values. However, I believe that we are only the custodians of this beautiful planet called earth. When we go in to the forest, or with permission, on to private property, it is important how we leave that land. It is only common sense and polite to carry out everything we bring in and even carry out any trash that we see, which may have been left by others.

As stewards of the land, particularly public land, I hope that everyone will advocate for continuing designation of wilderness areas and other set asides such as wildlife refuges. Wildlife is a renewable resource. Hunter dollars from fees and licenses have rejuvenated the numbers of some big game species such as white tailed deer to record levels. We need to continue all wildlife enhancement and restoration programs. Hunting should be retained not only as an accessible sport, but part of the plans to ensure that wild animals do not exceed the carrying capacity of the habitat.

I encourage everyone to get out and see the great outdoors. Here are some of the places we go to hunt. fish, camp and just chill out and do nothing. We are truly blessed!

Alaska, the last frontier!

Southwest Alaska

Oxbow Reservoir on the Snake River on the Oregon/Idaho border

Mt. Hood National Forest – Oregon's Cascade Mountains

Just for fun - Bigfoot; is it real?

In June of 2013 Donnell and I auditioned and were selected to compete as a team on an expedition to document the existence of the legendary creature known as Bigfoot or Sasquatch. Nine teams were selected.

There have been thousands of sightings of this mythical being. The Northwest, especially the mountains of Central Washington and Northern California, has recorded more sightings of Sasquatch than any other areas in the continental United States. Spike TV hired an Emmy Award winning director to lead the filming of this expedition to determine if a hairy, 8-foot primate, which has yet to be scientifically documented, really exists. We were hunting with only cameras, audio recorders, and kits to take samples of anything, which might contain DNA like hair, feces or bones. We went out without any weapons, not even a pocketknife.

Donnell and I have heard strange sounds on one of our big game hunts for deer and bear in the Mt. Hood National Forest in the Cascade Mountains of Central Oregon. However, I believe my theory about some the sightings, which I shared during the audition, may have lead to our selection to compete on this program, which was aired nationally on Spike TV in January and February of 2014. My theory was based Oregon and Northwest history.

On February 14, 1859, Oregon became the first state admitted to the Union with an exclusion law written into the state constitution. In 1862 Oregon adopted a law requiring all blacks, Chinese, Hawaiians, and Mulattos residing in Oregon to pay an annual tax of $5. If they could not pay this tax, they could be whipped and the law empowered the state to press them into service maintaining state roads for 50 cents a day. Interracial marriages between blacks and whites were banned in Oregon; it was against the law for whites to marry anyone ¼ or more black. In

1866 Oregon citizens did not pass the 14th Amendment, granting citizenship to blacks. The state's ban on interracial marriages was extended to prevent whites from marrying anyone who is ¼ or more Chinese or Hawaiian, and ½ or more Native American.

In 1926 Oregon repealed its exclusion law, amended the state constitution to remove it from the Bill of Rights. Finally, in 1927 the Oregon State Constitution was amended to remove a clause denying blacks the right to vote.

What do these history facts have to do with Bigfoot? Well I believe that it is possible that some of these sightings of tall dark primates could have been slaves, descendents of slaves or free people of African descent, who relocated to the Northwest from other areas of the country. In an effort avoid conflict with Oregon (California had some discriminatory practices as well) these people may have settled in the high mountains away from others and kept to themselves. Some of the alleged sightings of Bigfoot could have been tall black people wearing coats made of animal skins or hides. It just a theory and nobody agrees with me, but I think it helped us to get on Spikes TV's 10 Million Dollar Bigfoot Bounty

Does Bigfoot really exist? Well we were unable to prove it on this expedition. We hunted for the hairy beast on Mt Adams in central Washington. The weather was hot exceeding 90 degrees on most days. The altitude was 5,000 to 6,000 feet above sea level. We avoided any meetings with the Black bears, cougars and the Western Timber Rattlesnake. We won the first episode, but were given a quick exit to end the second program in the series. They brought us back for the10th episode, the finale. No one claimed the ten million dollar prize but one of the teams was awarded a $100,000 research grant that all the teams were competing for as well. This was a great experience. We learned more about hunting and made some good friends.

Donny and Donnell were known as Team Chocolate. I didn't have anything to with color. Donnell's middle name is Chocolate, which is his mother's birth or family name.

Team Chocolate with the TV host Dean Cain on Mt Adams in central Washington.

Surf and Turf

I never forget my roots in the outdoors, which is fishing. Often when we go on hunting trips there are also opportunities to get out the fishing gear and cast for a variety of species. As mentioned before I grew up on a few warm water species, but I have enjoyed adding new varieties of fish to the dinner table over the years. Along with bass, crappies, catfish, bluegill and perch up north; down south has alligator gar, stripped bass and drum. There are also larger and more species of catfish including, blue and spoonbill. I have caught trout in the northwest since my college days. Recently we have tried our hand at sturgeon and salmon as well.

I can recall one duck hunt with Donnell where we didn't get any ducks. However, when we arrived back at the dock some folks were catching crappie from the bank. We quickly got the boat on the trailer and grab our rods and reels. We caught about 25 fish that evening, then came back the next morning and really went to town. We caught at least 100 crappies.

During warm summer evenings it is great to drive a short cast from the metropolitan area to see if we can catch something for dinner. Last summer my wife Faye showed her country roots and started fishing again. Here is a nice largemouth bass she harvested at the Sauvie Island Wildlife Area, a state owned and managed preserve near our home in North Portland, Oregon.

Stampede

Years ago when Donnell (now 29 years old) was a toddler, Faye and I took him with us out to Sauvie Island for the "evening bite". We had been catching crappie from a footbridge across one of the interior lakes about a half-mile from the east side parking area. We had to walk through a herd of cows grazing the pasture. Earlier in the week when we came out, a couple of those young bulls were a little testy and challenged us as we walked the dirt road to this honey hole. We had walked just a few yards from the car when I said to Faye, "I don't like the way those cows were acting the other day. Let me get my pistol". After I retrieved my Ruger .22 Magnum revolver, which I still carry when I'm fishing 27 years later, we proceeded to the catwalk. There was one older Black gentleman already fishing there. He had few crappie and the fish were biting.

It was getting dark and we had some fish in the 5-gallon bucket. We started walking back down the dirt road to the car. After a few minutes the old guy also left. He took a short-cut crossing the field south of us and stampeded about 60 cows toward us! I had no choice but to pull my gun and shoot it in the air. I instantly flashed back to my days as a kid watching the TV show Rawhide. One shot. Nothing happened. They were still charging toward us. Two shots. The thundering herd turned a little. With each shot my aim went lower. On the third shot the herd of cows finally turned north so we could head east to the parking lot. When we got there, the old man was waiting. "Y'all all right" he said. "Ah yeah. No thanks to you sir". "I'm sorry", he said. No cows or people were injured thank God.

We laugh about this incident now, almost every time Faye and I go fishing. "You remember that stampede?" she will say. "Yep, we almost literally bit the dust." Haha!

Final thoughts

Thank you for letting me share my experiences and thoughts about hunting with you. There are many sources of information on hunting, shooting and related outdoor recreation. You should use the great volume and quality of information on the Internet and hunting magazines are a good source of information. The hunting media has been slow to embrace diversity and inclusion, but a few articles from and about African American hunters are being published. One such article, which we believe may have been the first on the topic of Black hunters, was published in Outside Magazine in November 2010. The article, Cool Hunter, written by Michael J. Mooney, profiled the efforts of African American Hunting Association, LLC to encourage Black people to consider hunting. It was a thorough 4-page article reviewing the past, present and future of Black hunters.

Donnell Chocolate Adair as seen in Outside Magazine

We took some young folks on an upland bird hunt after shooting lessons at the Portland Gun Club

Donnell and Eugene Anderson of Oakland, California met while attending the University of Oregon. They and other young men and women represent the future of hunting. When and where will you find your next hunting partner? We'll see you in the field!

Hunting and Shooting Resources

African American Hunting Association, LLC
Donny Adair, President
donnyadair@yahoo.com (503) 515-9853
https://www.facebook.com/pages/African-American-Hunting-Association/
aahunt.com or africanamericanhunting.com

African American Gun Association
http://www.naaga.co/#african-american-firearm-fishing-and-outdoors-clubs

Urban American Outdoors - Kansas City, Mo

African American Gun Club - Atlanta, Ga.

Dorie Miller Rifle and Pistol Club - Buffalo, New York

Black Wolf Hunting Club
http://campingincolor.blogspot.com/

Outdoor Afro
http://www.outdoorafro.com

Black Gun Owners
http://www.blackgunowners.org

Bigdeerhunters.com

Black Gun Owners and Hunters Online

Black People Fishing and Hunting - Facebook

Printed in the United States
By Bookmasters